Alfred Austin

**A Vindication of Lord Byron**

Alfred Austin

**A Vindication of Lord Byron**

ISBN/EAN: 9783743346451

Manufactured in Europe, USA, Canada, Australia, Japa

Cover: Foto ©ninafisch / pixelio.de

Manufactured and distributed by brebook publishing software
(www.brebook.com)

Alfred Austin

**A Vindication of Lord Byron**

# A VINDICATION

OF

# LORD BYRON.

BY

## ALFRED AUSTIN.

" La fiera moglie più ch'altro mi nuoce."—DANTE.
" More than all else hurts me my cold proud spouse."

LONDON :

CHAPMAN AND HALL, 193, PICCADILLY.

1869.

# PREFACE.

What may be called the skeleton of the following Vindication appeared in the columns of an influential daily newspaper at the time that the controversy raised by Mrs. Stowe's article in *Macmillan's Magazine* had just commenced. As will readily be comprehended, I was not quite a free agent either in the matter of space or time; and though all *Byroniana* have been with me a study ever since my first recollection of men and books, I was not able, within the limits imposed, to do anything like full justice to the subject. This I have striven to accomplish in the ensuing pages.

It will be perceived that I entertain no doubt whatever as to Mrs. Stowe's good faith, however ill I may think of her judgment. Of all incredible things, nothing is so incredible as that Lady Byron did not in substance tell her the story she in turn has told to us. But if Lady Byron told her the story, and the story is proved to be untrue in its entirety, and in many particulars utterly impossible, what becomes of Lady Byron's credibility as a witness on the subject at all?

This is a highly important question, seeing that those who desire to depreciate Byron's name and fame, now that they are beginning to discover that incest cannot be proved against him, are changing their tactics, and commencing to harp upon his cruelty. But who says he was cruel? Lady Byron, and Lady Byron only—the same person who asserts that he was guilty of incest, and that she herself took charge of the child which was the result of his sin !

Even supposing that Lady Byron's value as a witness was not thus under a cloud, why should she be believed rather than Lord Byron? On account of his general " immorality," in the ordinary sense of that term ? If so, the word of the average woman must be much more trustworthy than that of the average man. Yet, is it? Everybody knows that it is not, and that "immorality" and untruthfulness have no connection, either essential or inferential. Lord Byron's credibility, therefore, would be quite equal to that of Lady Byron, even if hers remained excellent. After the discredit into which it has now fallen, his must, by all the laws of impartiality, be taken to be considerably superior.

Such being the case, let us select the following as a crucial test of the charge of cruelty. Lady Byron says that it commenced the moment she quitted the altar with her husband. She has given two accounts of what occurred, and here they both are. The first is the one she gave to Mrs. Stowe :—

> " The moment the carriage doors were shut upon the bridegroom and bride the paroxysm of remorse and despair—unrepentant remorse and angry despair—broke forth upon her gentle head. ' You might have saved me from all this, madam ! You had it all in your own power when I offered myself to you first. Then you might have made me what you pleased; but now you will find that you have married a *devil.*' "

This, we say, was the account narrated by Lady Byron herself to Mrs. Stowe. The following is the one which, again, Lady Byron herself narrated to Lady Anne Barnard :—

> " They had not been an hour in the carriage which conveyed them from the church when, breaking into a malignant sneer, ' Oh, what a dupe you have been to your imagination ! How is it possible a woman of your sense could form the wild hope of reforming *me ?* Many are the tears you will have to shed ere that plan is accomplished. It is enough for me that you are my wife to hate you; if you were the wife of any other man I might own you had charms.' "

Now I should have very much liked to see either Sir Samuel Romilly or Dr. Lushington, who both so readily believed whatever it may happen to have been that Lady Byron told them, with a witness under cross-examination who had given two such contradictory accounts of the same transaction as are contained in the above extracts.

Why, such evidence, if brought against a pickpocket, would ensure his acquittal! Yet it is upon this testimony that we are invited to believe that Byron's sister—never before arraigned before any tribunal, and hitherto supposed to be an angel of "sweetness and light"—was guilty of adultery and incest, and Byron himself of both these offences, linked with brutal cruelty, life-long hypocrisy—in fact, with every foul sin and mean crime under heaven.

It so happens, however, that some such story as one of the above—perhaps some different one again—did reach Lord Byron's ears, and these are his recorded comments upon it :—

"I was surprised at the arrangements for the journey, and somewhat out of humour to find the lady's-maid stuck between me and my bride. It was rather too early to assume the husband; so I was forced to submit, but it was not with a good grace. I have been accused of saying, on getting into the carriage, that I had married Lady B. out of spite, and because she had refused me twice. Though I was for a moment vexed at her prudery, or what you may choose to call it, if I had made so uncavalier, not to say so brutal a speech, I am convinced Lady Byron would instantly have left the carriage to me and the maid. She had spirit enough to have done so, and would properly have resented the affront. Our honeymoon was not all sunshine; it had its clouds."

The individual who arbitrarily rejects this statement and arbitrarily selects for belief one of Lady Byron's various different statements, must be constitutionally incapable of weighing evidence, or be of the settled opinion that accusation of guilt is equivalent to proof of it.

Many people regret that this question has been opened at all. For my part, I rejoice at it. "There will come a day of reckoning," Byron wrote to Mr. Murray from Bologna in 1819, "even if I should not live to see it." It appears to me that day has come. That Byron was sadly "sinning," no one would dream of denying; but he was shockingly "sinned against"—and now, thank God! we know it.

*September* 10, 1869.

To the Memory of

BYRON'S "SWEET SISTER"

I INSCRIBE

THIS VINDICATION

OF HER NAME

AND

HER FATHER'S IMMORTAL SON.

*Man.*—And what are they who do avouch these things ?
*Abbot.*—* * Pious brethren * * *
　　　Even thine own vassals.—*Manfred.*


I have had many foes, but none like thee ;
　For 'gainst the rest myself I could defend,
　And be avenged, or turn them into friend ;
But thou, in safe implacability,
Hast nought to dread.
*　　*　　*　　*　　*　　*

And thus upon the world—trust in thy truth,
And the wild fame of my ungoverned youth—
　On things that were not and on things that are—
Even upon such a basis hast thou built.
*　　*　　*　　*　　*　　*

But of thy virtues didst thou make a vice,
*　　*　　*　　*　　*　　*

And buying others' grief at any price.
And thus once entered into crooked ways,
The early truth, which was thy proper praise,
Did not still walk beside thee—but at times,
And with a breast unknowing its own crimes,
Deceits, averments incompatible,
Equivocations *　　*　　*　　*
*　　*　　*　　*　　*　　*

All found a place in thy philosophy.
　The means were worthy, and the end is won ;
　I would not do by thee as thou hast done.
　　　　*Lines on Hearing that Lady Byron was Ill.*
　　　　　　*September,* 1816.

# A VINDICATION OF LORD BYRON.

FIVE-AND-FORTY years ago a poet died in the cause of freedom at Missolonghi, whom Macaulay, with appropriate pomp of language, has called "the most illustrious Englishman of the nineteenth century." During the brief space of manhood that was allotted to him—only sixteen years in all—he kept the world hanging upon the accents of his lyre. Master of all moods, he had his generation attentive at his feet; and even the philosophic Goethe, who alone among modern men of letters could pretend to be his peer, declared him to be the greatest human product the world has ever seen, or is likely to see. In times nearer to our own, this applause of applauded men has not been echoed by those whose endorsement would scarcely increase its authority. Literary criticism has long been dead amongst us, and the current opinions of fashionable conventionality have fondly attached themselves to the more feminine and academical verse of their own smaller day. Yet the comparatively silent but sounder portion of the public voice has all along steadfastly clung to the higher and better judgments we have cited ; and we feel fully assured that the declaration made by Goethe on another occasion—that " the wonderful glory to which Byron has in the present, and through all future ages, elevated his country, will be as boundless in its splendour as it is incalculable in its consequences ; nor can there be any doubt that the nation which boasts so many great names will class Byron among the first of those through whom she has acquired such glory "—embodies the definitive conclusion of every competent critic. There is one name below that does rival Shakespeare's, and it is his of whom the same great German has averred that " his unfathomable qualities are not to be reached by words."

But it was not by his writings alone that Byron became during life and after it a household word. He contracted an infelicitous marriage ; and his separation from his wife aroused as much excitement in the public mind as a couple of years before was wont to be manifested on the news of a fresh disaster of Buonaparte's, or the tidings of a fresh victory by Wellington. The attitude of the world on the occasion has been portrayed by the most brilliant of English essayists in one of the most epigrammatic passages he ever wrote, and its sentences are too familiar to need reproduction or imitation here.

Though the whole world was dying to know the cause of the separation, not a soul was able to fathom it. Lord Byron publicly asserted that he was himself completely in the dark on the subject; while Lady Byron at the time refused to communicate her knowledge, save to a couple of lawyers, on whose lips she set the solemn seal of silence. People were thus left to their own surmises, and these naturally varied with the temper which undertook to solve the insoluble out of the depths of its own consciousness. It is enough to say that whilst the uncharitable, the inexperienced, and the prurient attributed to Lord Byron unutterable things, sensible men of the world came to the conclusion that there was nothing to solve; that what is called incompatibility of temper, an imperfect fidelity on the part of the husband, and an exacting jealousy on the part of the wife, had conspired to put asunder a couple who never ought to have been joined together. Great compassion was always felt for the lady, for no one could pretend that Byron was likely to make an exemplary husband; and considerable sympathy was always felt for the man, because he was superlatively gifted, had bestowed on his race immortal verse, and in more discreet or less exacting hands

> " Might still have risen from out the grave of strife,
> And found a nobler duty than to part."

Forty-five years after the death of the husband, and

nine after that of the wife, during all which time not a word was ever authoritatively uttered to solve what some still declared to be a mystery, but what the majority believed to be no mystery at all, but only a mystification —an American authoress, who is known to the public by a clever but uncandid romance, has been permitted by the editors of what has hitherto been thought a respectable magazine to tell in its pages what she calls "The True Story of Lady Byron's Life." She does so, she affirms, on the authority of Lady Byron herself, who, four years before her death, made her the *confidante* of the real cause of the separation. She adds that Lady Byron, besides recounting the history which is embodied in the article, showed the writer of it a paper containing a brief memorandum of the whole, with the dates affixed.

Now I am not going to allow the authoress of "Uncle Tom's Cabin" to employ over again in these pages the well-known dexterity of the romance writer, when fiction has to be made to look like fact. I shall state Mrs. Stowe's "True Story" in a much more naked form than that in which she, with her novelist's skill, instinctively felt it would be wise to state it, if it was ever to carry conviction to those who read it. I shall suppress none of her language, but I shall add some plainer and more unvarnished language of my own.

Mrs. Beecher Stowe's statement, then, professedly

taken from Lady Byron's own lips and handwriting, is
that the real causes of her separation from Lord Byron
were that he had formed an adulterous and incestuous
intrigue with his half-sister Augusta, the wife of Colonel
Leigh; that in the very first hours of his marriage with
Lady Byron he informed her that his soul was the deposi-
tory of a dreadful secret of guilt, and torn with agonies of
remorse; that she might have saved him from it had she
accepted him when he first proposed to her; that then
she might have made of him what she pleased, but that
now she would find she had married a devil; that there
came an hour of revelation—note the melodramatic language and the total absence of any reference to a date—
when Lady Byron was made acquainted by Lord Byron
of this incestuous and adulterous connection, and was
told by him that he would on no account abandon it;
that he had married her simply that she might be the
cloak and accomplice of this atrocious passion; that on
hearing such a disclosure Lady Byron neither fled from
him, nor exposed nor denounced the crime; that she was
resolved neither to leave nor to betray him; that she
struggled with him convulsively for two years—again
mark the melodramatic inaccuracy as to facts, for Lord
and Lady Byron's real married life consisted altogether
not of two years, but of one year and a fortnight exactly!
—that Lord Byron argued the case with her with all the
sophistries of his powerful mind, tried to destroy her faith

in right and wrong, to persuade her of the just claim
of every human being to follow out what he called the
impulses of nature, and to bring her to accept the
marriage-tie as a friendly alliance to cover licence, both
on his part and on hers; that he could extract from her
neither anger, scorn, loathing, threats, nor compliance,
but only the stereotyped and long-suffering answer, " I
am too truly your friend to do this ; " that when he found
he had to do with one who would not yield, he determined to get rid of her altogether; that he did get rid of
her; that Lady Byron did not leave her husband, but
was by cruelty driven from him; that he drove her from
him in order to follow up the guilty infatuation which
was consuming him ; that having done so, he went
abroad, never seeing his sister again because Lady Byron
made it a condition—a condition of what, is not stated
—that the unhappy partner of his sin should not follow
him out of England, but that the ruinous intrigue should
be given up ; that all the beautiful, tender, and pathetic
verse, and all the letters he ever penned upon the subject,
were part and parcel of a deliberate and life-long hypocrisy; that he hated Lady Byron with undying hate, and
that the enmity which, it is asserted, was constantly
expressing itself in some publication or other, arose from
her inflexible resolve that he and his sister should be
separated ; that he remained impenitent and implacable
on this point to the hour of his death ; that Lady Byron

loved her husband with "deep affection and divine charity," manifesting "intense faithfulness and love" to his memory to the very last; and that always, and ever before her, during the few remaining years of her widowhood—mark, again, the melodramatic hand; the *few* remaining years of her widowhood were thirty-six, exactly as long (strange coincidence!) as her husband's entire life—was the image of Lord Byron purified and ennobled, "the angel in him made perfect, according to the divine ideal."

Such is the substance of the "True Story" related in *Macmillan's Magazine* for the current month by the authoress of "Uncle Tom's Cabin." I have no hesitation in declaring that in the mind of any one even decently capable of examining and sifting evidence, it is the most preposterous fable that was ever attempted to be foisted by mingled hallucination and credulity on the curiosity of the public.

Not to dwell at present upon the obvious inconsistencies contained in the above long catalogue of statements, nearly every one of them is, *à priori*, so intensely improbable, that nothing but absolute demonstration would make any sane and unbiassed person believe it implicitly; and all of them, when taken together, constitute a cumulative improbability so enormous that no person, unless the most credulous creature in the world, could think of believing it at all.

Indeed, it is enough to array them side by side to discredit them. Even probable stories must be consistent, but what credence can be given by any man in his senses to stories that are grossly improbable and grossly inconsistent as well? For the "True Story" to be even credible, it ought to have run thus. Byron maintained an incestuous intrigue with his sister, and Lady Byron found it out. She then either left him at once, or as soon after as he had flatly refused to promise that it should be given up. He did refuse, and she left him. He then renewed the incestuous connection; or he abandoned it and held his peace for the remainder of his life through fear of his wife denouncing him. This, we say, though an uncommonly improbable story, would hang together in a fashion; but still there would have been difficulties in the way of its acceptance, which to our thinking would be insuperable. To begin with, and granting the guilt of the lovers, discovery by the wife would not be very likely; and, in the second place, discovery, if attended with an offer of condonation, would have been sure to bring at least feigned repentance. Even then the fact would still remain, that not feigning repentance, Lord Byron lost no opportunity of parading his wrongs and calling upon his wife to speak out. But this story, difficult as it would be to believe it, is not the story at all. How infinitely more incredible still it is, we have seen.

Having thus paused to mark the probability of this narrative when taken in its entirety, let us now examine its principal statements in detail.

What evidence have we of the terrible charge now made, for the first time, against Lord Byron and his sister? None whatever, but Mrs. Stowe's assertion of Lady Byron's assertion, made thirty-two years after the death of the first, and seventeen years after the death of the second. What is the evidence against it? Let us see; for it happens to be very considerable.

In 1812, as all the world knows, the first two cantos of "Childe Harold" were published, and it was by virtue of their success that Byron woke up one morning, as he said, and found himself famous. This was three years before his marriage, and two, according to Mrs. Beecher Stowe's account, before he commenced the incestuous intrigue with his sister, who had already been married five years, and was the Honourable Mrs. Leigh. To her one of the first presentation copies of "Childe Harold" was sent, and in it, if the volume has not been destroyed by the accusers of the fair fame of each, may to this day be read the following inscription, in Byron's handwriting :—

"To Augusta, my dearest sister and my best friend, who has loved me much better than I deserved, this volume is presented by her father's son, and most affectionate brother."

In a letter written to the *Times*, it has been said that

the gallantries of Augusta's mother, Baroness Conyers, were so notorious, and the absences from home of her husband, Captain Byron, so frequent, that probably Lord Byron and the Honourable Mrs. Leigh did not regard each other as brother and sister at all. This may be taken as a fair sample of the inexact comments that have been made on the subject during the last few weeks. For nothing can be made more clear, as will be seen, than that Byron regarded Mrs. Leigh as peculiarly his sister from her goodness to him, and loved to call her by that title, which he regarded as the highest and purest of all. We have just seen one instance. Let us now look at some others. In his journal, dated the 28th of March, 1814, occurs the following entry :—

" Augusta wants me to make it up with Carlisle. I have refused everybody else, but I can't deny her anything ; so I must e'en do it, though I had as lief ' drink up Eisel, eat a crocodile.' "

In a letter written about a month earlier, from Newstead, to Mr. Murray, he says incidentally :—" Mrs. Leigh is with me—much pleased with the place, and less so with me for parting with it, to which not even the price can reconcile her. Your parcel has not yet arrived—at least the magazines, &c." Six days later he writes to Moore :—" I arrived in town late yesterday evening, having been absent about three weeks, which I passed in Notts "—at Newstead, and also at Colonel Leigh's, that is—" quietly and pleasantly." No references could well be more natural; yet they were penned just about the time that Mrs. Stowe intimates the incestuous passion commenced, *i.e.*, shortly after Lady Byron refused his first offer, and he himself had entered in his journal, "A wife would be the salvation of me." On the 18th of July of the same year we come across the following P.S. in a letter to Mr. Murray :—

"If you could spare the *Edinburgh Review* for an hour in the evening, I wish you to send it up to Mrs. Leigh, your neighbour, at the London Hotel, Albemarle Street."

On the 24th he writes to the same correspondent concerning the well-known portrait of him done by Phillips, in this strain :—

"For my own part, I have no objection at all; but Mrs. Leigh and my cousin must be better judges of the likeness than others; and they hate it; and so I won't have it at all."

"Mrs. Leigh and my cousin." As we shall more than once have occasion to remark, he was a firm believer in "cousinship" and all ties of blood. On the 2nd of January of the following year, as everybody knows, he was married. On the 8th of March he says in a letter to Moore :—

"We leave this place"—his father-in-law's—"to-morrow, and shall stop on our way to town (in the interval of taking a house there) at Colonel Leigh's, near Newmarket, where any epistle of yours will find its welcome way."

The next testimony of his affection for his sister that we may cite was his desire that his daughter should be called after her. She is best known by the name of Ada, in consequence of the famous line—

" Ada, sole daughter of my house and heart ! "

but her complete name was Augusta Ada ; and, whilst we are thus presented with the astounding fact that Lady Byron knowingly allowed her own child to be called after the name of her husband's incestuous paramour, we discern another proof of Byron's loving attachment even to the very name of his sister.

Augusta Ada Byron was born on the 10th of December, 1815 :—" The little girl," Byron wrote to Moore, " was and is very flourishing and fat, and reckoned very large for her days—squalls and sucks incessantly. Her mother is doing very well, and up again."

By the middle of January it was all over. Lady Byron refused even to see her husband again, or, as Mrs. Stowe puts it, had been purposely driven away by him. On the 25th of April—not till more than three months later—Byron quitted England. Concerning Mrs. Stowe's assertion that Lady Byron made it a condition—as I have observed, she does not say a condition of what—that the partner of his guilt should not accompany him to the Continent, I shall have a word more to say anon. But on the 16th of April, or nine days before his departure, I find Byron writing this short note to Rogers :—

" My sister is now with me, and leaves town to-morrow. We shall not meet again for some time at all events, if ever ; and, under these circumstances, I trust to stand excused to you and Mr. Sheridan for being unable to wait upon him this evening."

Moore adds, in the " Life ":—" This was his last interview with his sister—almost the only person from whom he now parted with regret ; it being, as he said, doubtful which had given him most pain, the enemies who attacked, or the friends who condoled with him." I put it to anybody if there is in the foregoing note, written at such a crisis, anything to bear out the shocking story told by Mrs. Stowe, and not, on the contrary, everything to make belief in it impossible. Where are the secret guilt, the agony of soul, the remorse, the " insane fear of detection," which she says marked all his words and actions in this matter ? His sister does not frantically stay with him to the last moment ; his parting with her takes place nine days before he sails ; and his allusion to this last interview is precisely what one would expect from an affectionate brother, and nothing more.

He went abroad ; and what are henceforward the recorded mentions that he made of this cherished sister ? Writing to Mr. Murray from Venice, on the 2nd of January, 1817, he says, among a number of other things :—" I have received a letter from my sister, written on the 10th of December, my daughter's birthday (and relative chiefly to my daughter)."

On the 3rd of March he writes thus to the same correspondent :—

"Ever since the conclusion of the Carnival I have been unwell (do not mention this on any account to Augusta, for if I grow worse she will know it too soon, and if I get better there is no occasion she should know it at all)."

The "on no account" seems, however, to have been a mere *façon de parler*, such as we all of us employ so often, and to have been disregarded ; for in another letter shortly afterwards, to the same correspondent, I find him writing :—

"I have had another letter from my poor dear Augusta, who is in a sad fuss about my late illness; do pray tell her (the truth) that I am better than ever, and in importunate health, growing (if not grown) large and ruddy, and congratulated by impertinent persons on my robustious appearance, when I ought to be pale and interesting."

In 1821, after the first two cantos of " Don Juan " had been published, he thus frankly records his sister's attitude towards that poem—a striking testimony to the, some will think, excessive squeamishness of one whom we are invited to regard as the most impure and degraded of her sex :—

"Augusta writes that they are thought '*execrable*' (bitter word *that* for an author—eh, Murray ?) as a *composition* even, and that she had heard so much against them that she would never read them, *and never has*. Be that as it may, I can't alter ; that is not my forte."

This is the last reference I find to her, save his remembrance of her in his will; and the person who can make anything out of these passages but easy and beautiful brotherly love, must be determined to believe an unpleasant story at all costs, the cost of evidence included. Her name, together with that of " my wife— Ada—Hobhouse—Kinnaird—Greece," was on his dying lips. He would not have been the brother we take him for, if it had not been; and it is evident from the mention of Hobhouse and Kinnaird that he was thinking of " poor Augusta's " narrow means, and recommending her to Lady Byron's kindness—of which more anon.

So much for prose testimony on this head. Let me now turn to verse, since Mrs. Stowe has availed herself of " Manfred" and " Cain" to support her story, and has done it in a way that does little credit to the purity of her imagination. Were I not speaking of a woman, I should express myself more strongly. She quotes a passage from " Cain," with the object of showing that its author strove to argue that incest is no sin. I need not reproduce it here. Neither need I reproduce all that was said for and against " Cain " when it first appeared. But Byron himself wrote pages on pages in vindication of it, and one brief extract from them must content me. It occurs in a letter to Mr. Murray :—

" As to ' alarms,' do you really think such things ever led anybody astray? Are these people more impious than Milton's Satan, or the Prometheus of Æschylus? Are not Adam, Eve, Adah, and Abel as pious as the catechism? I beg leave to observe that there is no creed nor personal hypothesis of mine in all this, but I was obliged to make Cain and Lucifer talk consistently, and surely this has always been permitted to poetry."

When I add that "Cain" was dedicated to Sir Walter Scott, who wrote to Mr. Murray:—

"I accept, with feelings of great obligation, the flattering proposal of Lord Byron to prefix my name to his very grand and tremendous drama. . . . . He certainly has matched Milton on his own ground. . . . . They must condemn the "Paradise Lost" if they intend to be consistent. . . . .",

I think I may dismiss the nasty charge that it contains a defence of incest.

The way in which Mrs. Stowe tries to turn "Manfred" to account deserves, if possible, to be still more warmly stigmatised. She would lead the ignorant reader to suppose that Byron, quitting England with the cherished guilt and heavy punishment of incest uppermost in his thoughts, forthwith composed "Manfred," the mystery of which, she avers, plainly turns upon that crime; and with an inaccurate audacity to which I in vain seek for a parallel, she affirms that "anybody who reads the tragedy of 'Manfred' with this story"—*i.e.*, her true story of Lady Byron's life—"in his mind, will see that it is true." We must observe, firstly, that, far from "Manfred" being the first work Byron composed after leaving England, both the third canto of "Childe Harold," and the

"Prisoner of Chillon," which even the authoress of "Uncle Tom's Cabin" would find it difficult to argue have any reference to incest, were written before it, along with various minor pieces. The precise value of the argument that if an allusion to incest can be construed out of any passage of "Manfred," everybody must see that Mrs. Stowe's story is true, and that Byron must have committed incest with his sister, may be dismissed with the remark that if it is good for anything, it is good to show that Byron committed murder as well; or, at least, that if Lady Byron, through Mrs. Stowe, chooses to say so, we shall be obliged to believe it. Whilst, with a strategy not usually considered commendable, Mrs. Stowe cites passages from "Manfred" utterly irrelevant to her particular accusation, but strongly calculated to impress upon the reader the conviction that the Manfred represented was capable of any and every crime, and that Lord Byron and Manfred are one, she abstains from quoting the particular passage to which we refer, and which runs as follows :—

*Manfred.*—I lov'd her and destroyed her.
*Witch.*—                    With thy hand ?
*Manfred.*—Not with my hand, but heart, which broke her heart ;
          It gazed on mine and withered. *I have shed*
          *Blood, but not hers—and yet her blood was shed ;*
          *I saw, and could not stanch it.*

Possibly Mrs. Stowe believes that Lord Byron was a

murderer, but she would be at a loss to show any reason whatever for thinking so, and even her own fabulous account of poor Mrs. Leigh bears testimony to the fact that she at least was murdered neither by her brother nor by anybody. And yet " anybody who reads the tragedy of ' Manfred' with this story in his mind, will see that it is true !" Again we say that such a strange instance of a person zealously playing the part of "devil's-advocate" was never before known.

Although we have no fear that anybody reading " Manfred " will arrive at the conclusion Mrs. Stowe, with fierce perversity, labours to enforce, it will be well, whilst on this part of the subject, to refer to another cock-and-bull story evolved out of " Manfred " by no less a person than Goethe ; for, in the first place, it will prove that "incest," at least, never entered Goethe's mind ; and, secondly, it will show how absolutely without bounds are the crimes that may be imputed to authors if we once adopt Mrs. Stowe's process of seeking in their works for a confirmation of affirmed enormities :—

"It is related," says Goethe, writing of "Manfred," "that Byron, when a bold and enterprising young man, won the affections of a Florentine lady. Her husband discovered the amour, and murdered his wife ; but the murderer the same night was found dead in the street, and there was no one to whom any suspicion could be attached. Lord Byron removed from Florence, and these spirits haunted him all his life after. This romantic incident is rendered highly probable by innumerable allusions to it in his poems," and, as we have seen, by the words of Manfred :—

> " I have shed
> Blood, but not hers—and yet her blood was shed ;
> I saw, and could not stanch it."

If Goethe had said of his story what Mrs. Stowe says of hers, that "anybody who reads the tragedy of 'Manfred' with this story in his mind will see that it is true," he would at least have had Manfred to justify him. Mrs. Stowe has absolutely nothing to justify her, save her incomprehensible feminine zeal.

Upon Goethe's "highly probable incident" Moore has the following remarks :—

> "The grave confidence with which the venerable critic traces the fancies of his brother poet to real persons and events, affords an amusing instance of the disposition so prevalent throughout Europe to picture Byron as a man of marvels and mysteries, as well in his life as in his poetry. The consequence is, so utterly out of truth and nature are the representations of his life and character long current upon the Continent, that it may be questioned whether the real flesh and blood hero of these pages—the social, practical, and, with all his faults and inconsistencies, English Lord Byron—may not, to the over-exalted imaginations of most of his foreign admirers, appear but an ordinary, unromantic, and prosaic personage."

In 1821 Byron first heard of this story of Goethe, and this is how he treats it, in writing to Moore :—

> "Pray, where did you get hold of Goethe's Florentine husband-killing story ? Upon such matters in general, I may say, with Beau Clincher, in reply to Errand's wife, 'Oh, the villain ! he has murdered my poor Timothy !' Clincher : 'Damn your Timothy ! I

tell you, woman, your husband has *murdered me*—he has carried away my fine jubilee clothes !' "

But for the supreme horror of Mrs. Stowe's story, it would deserve to be treated in the same tone of persiflage.

There are several references to " Manfred " in Byron's journal and letters. One extract from the latter may suffice, for it is crushing in its unpremeditated evidence. In a letter written from Ravenna to Mr. Murray, in August, 1821, just at the time that he had made a present of materials for his life to Moore, he writes :—

" With regard to additions, &c., there is a journal which you must get from Mrs. Leigh, of my journey in the Alps, which contains all the germs of ' Manfred.' "

On another occasion, four years earlier, he had written :—

" The germs of ' Manfred ' may be found in the journal which I sent to Mrs. Leigh, when I first went on the Dent de Jaman, &c., &c. . . . I have the whole scene of ' Manfred ' before me, as if it was but yesterday, and could point it out, spot by spot, torrent and all."

Could anything more clearly demonstrate that Mrs. Leigh was not previously in possession of the germs which, on the supposition of the "True Story," she was only too well acquainted with, and that whatever they were, there was nothing to conceal in them ?

I cannot leave this particular part of the subject without referring to the line taken on it by the *Saturday Review.* Mrs. Stowe, as I have said, does not distinctly state, but leaves the reader to suppose, that "Manfred" was the first work written by Byron after the separation from his wife. The *Saturday Review*, only too willingly misled by her, asserts it in so many words. The assertion is utterly untrue. The first works written by Byron after the separation were the third canto of "Childe Harold," the "Prisoner of Chillon," and the "Monody on Sheridan." His intervals of leisure were spent in studying the Armenian grammar. The *Saturday Review*, vituperating —as a matter of course—both Mrs. Stowe and Lord Byron, says that the former cannot be at the trouble to spell Lady Byron's maiden name correctly. That is perfectly true ; but the *Saturday Review* cannot be at the trouble to learn Mrs. Leigh's mother's maiden name correctly at all. It calls her Lady Carnarvon, instead of Lady Caermarthen. That, of course, is a small matter, except in the case of such mighty critics. Would, however, that the *Saturday Review* had fallen into no more lamentable errors than that! I have already pointed out its misstatements in regard to "Manfred." Equally gross, and perhaps still graver, inaccuracy remains behind. It says that Byron in 1814 gave Moore a song, "which was never published till after the death of the former," and "which at this time seems significant." The song in question was the beautiful one beginning :—

"I speak not, I trace not, I breathe not thy name."

The origin of the song was as follows :—

"Dear Tom,—Thou hast asked for a song, and I enclose you an experiment, which has cost me something more than trouble, and is, therefore, less likely to be worth your taking any trouble in setting. Now, if it be so, throw it into the fire without phrase."

"Yours ever,          "BYRON."

In a note, Moore says, "I had begged of him to write something for me to set to music." The whole of this simple explanation, with which it is difficult to believe it was not acquainted, the *Saturday Review* suppresses; the song is garbled, just as are all the other quotations bearing, or supposed to bear, on the point; and the remark is then made, that the song *now*—*i.e.*, after Mrs. Stowe's story—is "significant!" I am aware that honourable and accomplished men have occasionally contributed to the *Saturday Review*. Still I feel confident that public opinion will bear me out when I say that this most notorious, but least respected of English weekly journals, systematically makes capital out of nastiness and the depreciation of great names; and that had it not believed that Lord Byron and Mrs. Leigh were guilty of incest, I should have been as much surprised as if I had discovered a jackal rejecting offal.*

* The *Saturday Review* takes under its patronage an article in the *Temple Bar Magazine* for June. The only possible reason for doing so must be the malignity of that article. All that it really proves, however, is—what everybody knew before—that Byron was

Just one word of protest before I resume the thread
of my criticism, on the attempt made, be it where it may,
to prove a man guilty of crimes from the tone or context
of his works.   Nothing can be more unfair or more
uncritical.  Some of my readers are probably aware of the
imputations which certain critics have brought against
Shakespeare, arising out of constructions they conceive
may be put on some of his sonnets.   These imputations
I indignantly repudiate ; but had Shakespeare's wife—to
whom we know he was not particularly attached—only
made the abominable charge the imputations involve, and
had she chosen further to communicate it to a contemporary
authoress like Mrs. Stowe, the latter's seventeenth century analogue would certainly have argued that anybody
who read the Sonnets with her story in his mind would
see that the story was true !   In Byron's case, the trouble
he took—like St. Augustine before his conversion—to
make himself out worse than he was, joined to "the wild
fame of his ungoverned youth," disposes many people to
believe anything and everything that can be said against
him ; and they are just as ready to convict him out of
his own writings as they would on the evidence of their

not a man of pure morals, and had an incurable habit of levity
both in speaking and writing.  In it "incest" is plainly hinted
at, and no wonder.  The writer of it is an attorney.  *Whose* attorney,
I leave my reader to surmise.  In fact, the conspiracy against Lord
Byron's reputation is a deeper one than has yet been fully ferreted
out.

own senses. Yet let them but look at the way in which he
continually tries to mystify people, and then declares that
he has been laughing at them! The following are quotations taken at random up and down his journals and
letters :—

"Last night I finished Zuleika"—the "Bride of Abydos," that
is—"my second Turkish tale. I believe the composition of it kept
me alive, for it was written to drive away the thoughts of," &c. . . .
"The 'Bride of Abydos' was written in four nights to distract my
dreams from . . . . Were it not thus, it had never been composed;
and had I not done something at the time, I should have gone mad
by eating my own heart—bitter diet . . . . I awoke from a dream!
—well! and have not others dreamed? Such a dream! but she
did not overtake me. I wish the dead would rest, however. . . . .
No dreams last night of the dead nor the living. . . . . Hobhouse
told me an odd report—that *I* am the actual Conrad, the veritable
Corsair. Um! people sometimes hit near the truth, but never the
whole truth. H. don't know what I was about, the year after he
left the Levant; nor does any one—nor—nor—nor—however, it is a
lie; but 'I doubt the equivocation of the friend that lies like
truth.'"

The person who can make anything out of the foregoing passages, much more believe that they faithfully
refer to actual incidents, must be—let us write it plainly
—an ass; the ass Byron intended to make of him.

When he was serious he wrote very differently :—

"The fools think," he says in a letter to Mr. Murray, "that all
my *poeshie* is always allusive to my own adventures; I have had
at one time or another better and more extraordinary, and perilous,
and pleasant than these every day of the week, if I might tell them :
but that must never be."

Yet, according to Mrs. Stowe and the *Saturday Review*, he has done it in four different poems, and various smaller pieces!

Still more expository of the real truth of the matter are two or three sentences in a letter to Moore, written from Ravenna in 1821 :—

> "I suppose I told you that the Giaour story had actually some foundation in facts. However, the *real* incident is still remote enough from the *poetical* one, being such as, happening to a man of imagination, might suggest such a composition. The worst of any *real* adventures is that they involve living people."

After this I trust we shall hear no more of such nonsense as that horrible stories "must be true," because something like them may be unearthed from the compositions of the accused.

To return now to Mrs. Stowe and the use she has thought proper to make of Lord Byron's poetical compositions, in the strenuous attempt to convict him and his "dearest sister and best friend" of incest. I think that every one will acknowledge they recoil upon herself. Now, however, I will myself have recourse to his poetry, having already appealed to his prose, to establish affirmatively, by yet another method, that the notion of the relationship charged can be harboured only by minds whose state we do not like to describe. The *Times*, which at first swallowed "The True Story" whole, without the faintest attempt at criticism or consideration, concluded its observations by saying that a black mark must henceforward be affixed to certain of Byron's compositions, if indeed we are ever to look at the man's works again.   If, instead of penning this hasty language, the *Times* had taken the pains to read over the three poems addressed by Byron to Augusta, and which are the ones evidently alluded to, we cannot think such a remark would ever have appeared in its columns. Even if there were no other reasons to disbelieve this dreadful story—and, thank Heaven! they are legion; while the reasons on the other side are monstrous and contradictory to the last degree — I would fearlessly appeal to these poems in order to rebut the abominable accusation.   How does one begin ?—

> " *My sister, my sweet sister ! if a name*
>     *Dearer and purer were, it should be thine ;*
> Mountains and seas divide us, but I claim
>     No tears, but tenderness to answer mine.
> Go where I will, to me thou art the same—
>     A loved regret which I would not resign.
> There yet are two things in my destiny—
> A world to roam through and a home with thee.

> " The first were nothing ; had I still the last,
>     It were the haven of my happiness ;
> *But other claims and other ties thou hast,*
>     *And mine is not the wish to make them less.*
> A strange doom is thy father's son's, and past
>     Recalling, as it lies beyond redress.
> Reversed for him our grandsire's fate of yore—
> He had no rest at sea, nor I on shore."

Is not this the same hand, influenced by the same heart, which in the flush of its first triumph wrote the inscription in one of the earliest presentation copies of the first two cantos of " Childe Harold?" " To Augusta, my dearest sister and my best friend, who has loved me much better than I deserved, this volume is presented by her father's son, and most affectionate brother." In the poem it is the grandsire, in the prose inscription it is the sire, to whom he alludes as binding them together ; but it is always the strong tie, and the deep feeling of blood and kinship, the only one he can trust. Again he writes, in another of these poems to which a black mark is to be henceforth attached :—

> " When all around grew drear and dark,
>     And reason half withheld her ray,
>     And hope but shed a dying spark,
>         Which more misled my lonely way ;
>
> " When fortune changed and love fled far,
>     And hatred's shafts flew thick and fast,
>     Thou wert the solitary star,
>         That rose and set not to the last !
>
> " Oh ! blest be thine unbroken light !
>     That watched me as a seraph's eye,
>     And stood between me and the night,
>         For ever shining sweetly nigh.
>
> " But thou and thine shall know no blight,
>     Whatever fate on me may fall ;
>     For Heaven in sunshine will requite
>         The kind—and thee the most of all."

The third poem remains, and its tone is precisely
similar :—

> " From the wreck of the past, which hath perished,
>    Thus much I at least may recall,
>  It hath taught me that what I most cherished
>    Deserved to be dearest of all.
>  In the desert a fountain is springing,
>    In the wide waste there still is a tree,
>  And a bird in the solitude singing,
>    Which speak to my spirit of *thee*."

Turn to " Childe Harold," that third canto, as we
have said, which was the first thing he wrote after
quitting England for ever, and which alone would make
us not only amply forgive, but be deeply thankful to
those who drove him from it.   Who does not know the
lines commencing :—

> " The castle crag of Drachenfels " ?

They, too, are addressed to " My sister, my sweet sister,"
and he here speaks of her as " the one soft breast "

> " *Whose love was pure and far above disguise.*"

Hark, how he addresses her :—

> " I send the lilies given to me ;
>    Though long before thy hand they touch
>  I know that they must withered be ;
>    But yet reject them not as such,
>  For I have cherished them as dear
>    Because they yet may meet thine eye,

And guide thy soul to mine even here,
　When thou behold'st them drooping nigh,
And know'st them gathered by the Rhine,
　And offered from my heart to thine!'"

Is that the language of incestuous passion? Is that
the utterance of one degraded soul to another? Shame
on the man or woman who for a moment should think
so! It is the voice of one love, and one only—the love
in which there is no constraint, no inequality, no fear,
no tumult, no jealousy, no dread—the love of brother to
sister—and lilies are its emblem. This was the sole
sweet oasis in the life of one who, as has well been
said of him, "was inspired by the Genius of Pain."

One more quotation on this score, and we have done.
He once wanted a simile for peace, happiness, tranquil-
lity; and where did he find it?

"Clear, placid Leman! thy contrasted lake,
　With the wild world I dwelt in, is a thing
Which warns me with its stillness to forsake
　Earth's troubled waters for a purer spring.
　This quiet sail is as a noiseless wing
To waft me from distraction; once I loved
　Torn Ocean's roar, but thy soft murmuring
Sounds sweet as *if a sister's voice reproved*
*That I with stern delights should e'er have been so moved.*"

He never had but one sister, and yet his unquenchable
notion of Sister was of one who lures a brother from
"stern delights." He would perforce have associated

her with one who lured *to* them, if this horrible tale could for one moment be admitted.

If the reader will turn back to the catalogue of statements which I have said must one and all be believed if this "True Story" is to be accepted, I think he will see that they are one and all really disposed of by what I have already said. Not wishing in any respect to imitate Mrs. Stowe, but avoiding all side issues, I have grappled directly with the one new, specific accusation she has attempted to fasten on the memory of Byron; and in the full confidence that I shall be considered successfully to have rebutted it, I might well here dismiss the matter. But the charge is one of such infamy, and the issue raised is of such vast moment, that I think I am justified in yet begging for the attention of my readers whilst I very briefly show the further inaccuracies as to fact, and the ludicrous contradictions into which Mrs. Stowe, by the zeal that outruns discretion and even candour, has been betrayed. And I pray my readers to bear in mind, whilst following my observations, that Mrs. Stowe's account professes to be not a happy guess or a plausible statement as to the causes which led to the separation of Lord and Lady Byron, but the one true story, exact in every particular, taken down from the lips and copied from the handwriting of Lady Byron herself, in an interview which had all the solemnity of a death-bed avowal.

We have seen how, though Mrs. Stowe expressly states that Lady Byron gave her "a paper containing a brief memorandum of the whole, *with the dates affixed*," no dates are mentioned by her at all, and Lady Byron is represented as having struggled convulsively with her husband for two years, whereas in reality they were not united for two years, but only for one. Furthermore, she dwells with all the force in her power upon Lord Byron's "damning, guilty secret filling him with an insane dread of detection," and yet she represents him both as making this secret the subject of his dramas and himself the guilty hero of them, and then goading Lady Byron by every species of insult into exposing him. She declares that he communicated this guilty secret to his wife, that he strove by sophistries to justify his crime, to sap her belief in Christianity and in right and wrong, and to get her to accept marriage as a mere cloak for the freer indulgence of the sexual passions, and that she was "the only one fully understanding the deep and dreadful secrets of his life;" and yet she quotes against him a letter written to Mr. Murray only a few days before Lady Byron left him for ever, in which he says, "I am very glad that the handwriting was a favourable omen of the *morale* of the piece, but you must not trust to that, for my copyist would write out anything I desired, *in all the ignorance of innocence.*" The copyist was Lady Byron herself; and we are therefore invited to believe that she

had retained " the ignorance of innocence," in spite of
her having a " full understanding of the dreadful secret "
that he maintained an incestuous intrigue with his sister,
and though he was continually arguing with her that
there was no harm in it, and that one ought to follow out
the impulses of nature !  She pretends in one place that
he married Lady Byron as a cloak for a crime which she
elsewhere describes as a "guilty *secret ;*" in another, that
he married her for money ;* and in a third, that he did
not want to marry her at all, but that " he had sent the
letter in mere recklessness, had not really seriously
expected to be accepted, and that the discovery of the
treasure of affection which he had secured was like a
vision of a lost heaven to a soul in hell."  She quotes
his words about Ada :—

> " The child of love, though born in bitterness
> And nurtured in convulsion,"

and positively quotes them incorrectly, substituting convulsion*s* for convulsion, in order to fortify a story she

* Nothing can show more saliently the readiness of people to
believe anything against Byron than the way in which the *Times,*
for instance, when retiring from its original position of complete
dupe, still credited Mrs. Stowe's assertion of Byron marrying Miss
Milbanke for money and squandering her fortune in his amours,
and spoke of his " despicable meanness."  Nothing could be more
untrue.  We could fill pages with testimonies of Byron's economical
style of living and personal generosity when abroad.  Moreover, Lady
Noel did not die till 1822, nor Lady Byron come in for the family

tells about Byron coming suddenly into his wife's room
a day or two after the child's birth, and informing her,
with cruel and malicious untruth, that her mother was
dead; utterly unable to see from her blind partisanship,
firstly, that if Byron had done anything of the kind he
would scarcely have recorded it in a poem; secondly,
that "nurtured" does not describe the condition of a
child two days old; and, thirdly, that if the passage is
good to prove, which it no doubt is, that Ada was born
in bitterness and nurtured in convulsion—not convulsion*s*
—it is equally good to prove that she was "the child of
love," a fact utterly inconsistent with Mrs. Stowe's whole
story, and particularly with her marvellous statement as
to the first words addressed by Byron to his wife immediately after the marriage ceremony. Moreover, she
avers, at page 383, that had the melancholy remembrance of their separation been allowed to sleep, the
"True Story" would never have been published; at
page 394, her implied excuse for it is that cheap editions
of Byron's works have brought his writings into circula-
tion among the masses; and at page 396, that, looking
anxiously to see a memoir of Lady Byron appear after

estates and her £7,000 a year till that date, six years after the separation, when Sir Francis Burdett arranged all financial matters
between them. All the money of hers he then spent was spent on
Greece; and we should have imagined that the philanthropic wor-
shippers of his philanthropic wife need not have begrudged the
use thus nobly made of it.

her death, and none such appearing, she has performed the necessary task.

There still remain a few points to be considered ; and I cannot quit the subject without alluding to them. Mrs. Stowe, whilst constantly referring to Lord Byron's terrible remorse and agony of soul, strives to make it appear he was so wicked that he would probably make light of incest, and asserts that he argued with his wife in favour of " Continental latitude, the good-humoured marriage in which complaisant couples mutually agree to form the cloak for each other's infidelities." If she had been acquainted with a published letter written by Byron to Moore, from Venice, in March, 1817, she might have read the following passage :—

" The Italian ethics are the most singular ever met with. The perversion, not only of action, but of reasoning, is singular in the women. It is not that they do not consider the thing itself as wrong, and very wrong; but *love* (the *sentiment* of love) is not merely an excuse for it, but makes it an actual virtue, provided it is disinterested, and not a *caprice*."

Again he writes from Verona :—

" The state of morals in these parts is in some sort lax. A mother and son were pointed out at the theatre, as being pronounced by the Milanese world to be of the Theban dynasty. The narrator (one of the first men in Milan) seemed to be not sufficiently scandalised by the tie."

In another place he speaks of the " misplaced and amusing morality of the Italians," and adds :—

" There is no convincing a woman here that she is in the smallest degree deviating from the rule of right or the fitness of things in having an amoroso."

So much for Byron's own ethical opinions, whatever his conduct may have been. Mrs. Stowe next lays stress upon the fact that the letter shown by him to Lady Blessington was never sent. Again, had she been better informed, she would have known that he wrote many letters to his wife which he did not send, and others which he did, according to the humour he found himself in, and the estimate he formed, after he had written them, of their doing any good.

With regard to Byron's insane dread of exposure by Lady Byron, on which I have already dwelt, I would ask, in addition, how is it possible that between them there should have passed such a correspondence as did take place in 1820, which may be found in the "Life," vol. iii. p. 115? In it Byron offers, and presses upon her, a perusal of his memoirs. She refuses, and throws out what he calls, in reply, a mysterious menace which he cannot pretend to unriddle, imploring her to "anticipate the period of her intention," and speak out before he dies. Does this look like dread of discovery? It was her very silence that maddened him; and he was everlastingly trying to provoke her into breaking it.

Mrs. Stowe asserts that Byron was consumed by a devouring passion for his sister. If so, why did he leave

England? There is no shadow of pretence that Lady Byron insisted on his doing so.

Such are some of the many " averments incompatible " —to use Lord Byron's phrase, singularly prophetic—into which Mrs. Beecher Stowe, instructed by Lady Byron, has fallen, whilst endeavouring, with frantic ardour, as though engaged in a task of benevolence, to fasten upon one of the greatest men that ever lived, and likewise upon his sister, his sweet sister, the most indelible of stigmas and the most revolting of crimes. I have been sparing of strong language ; but I should be shrinking from my duty if I did not complete this part of my subject by giving expression to the opinion that both Mrs. Stowe and the editor of *Macmillan's Magazine* have by their conduct incurred, and will continue to incur. the reprobation of all right-minded people.

Do I then suppose that the " True Story " is a mere concoction of Mrs. Stowe's brain? Certainly not. I shall have something to say directly of Mrs. Stowe's value as a witness; but it is idle to argue, as some people who desire to burke the question have done, that Lady Byron told Mrs. Stowe no such terrible tale as she tells us. We do not for one moment believe Mrs. Stowe to be a wilful writer of untruths; and though she has undoubtedly added plentiful colouring of her own, the story she relates is so particular and circumstantial, that it must be in the rough the story Lady Byron wished her to believe. On Lady Byron's credibility we will pronounce anon; but before explaining and accounting for Lady Byron's state of mind on the subject, let us first glance at Mrs. Stowe's state of mind during the interview.

In several places she speaks of Lady Byron's qualities as divine, and in two places she distinctly compares her to Christ. She talks of her as the impersonation of conscience, as a vision of heaven, as a guardian angel, as possessing a supernatural power of moral divination, as placing people's hands in that of the Saviour, as having more divine strength of faith and love than ever existed in a woman, and as more like a blessed being detached from earth than an ordinary mortal. In this worshipping vein she discourses of her throughout; and it is plain, therefore, that she sat raptly credulous during the whole interview, listening as to the sacred words of a celestial revelation, and that it is vain to expect from her at the time any critical or even ordinarily cautious scrutiny of Lady Byron's manner and words, or any submission of them since to the ordeal of reason, consistency, or common sense. Just as little is to be hoped for from the other reckless accomplices in the publication of this "True Story," the conductors of *Macmillan's Magazine*, since "pure," "lofty," "divine," are the only epithets which they too think properly applicable to Lady Byron.

We must, therefore, fall back upon Lady Byron's

statements, as presented to us by them, and ask, Did Lady Byron really believe that her husband had an incestuous intrigue with his sister, that he refused to abandon it, and drove her from him because "she personated conscience," and in order that he might follow out the guilty passion that was consuming him? We believe that a time did come when Lady Byron did persuade herself of the truth of these horrible things; that this persuasion on her part was a complete hallucination; and having already shown that it could not be anything but hallucination, we will endeavour to explain how it grew up in her mind.

Mrs. Stowe does not pretend to fix the date when Lady Byron first believed it, but contents herself with the melodramatic assertion that "there came an hour of revelation," and that Lady Byron struggled convulsively for two years to cure her husband of his abominable passion. We are thus left with no information whatever as to when the revelation burst upon her, and are notoriously misinformed as to the length of time during which Lady Byron kept the revelation to herself. Yet Lady Byron is Mrs. Stowe's authority both for the inaccuracy, and for the vagueness as to the hour of revelation. Under these circumstances we must have recourse to our leading witness—Lady Byron herself— and see what else she has stated on the subject to other people, and on other occasions.

Mrs. Stowe's case really is that Lady Byron did not quit her husband on account of his guilty infatuation for his sister, but that he, on account of it, so treated her as to compel her to leave him; and this tallies with the assertion made by Lady Byron in her written remarks on Moore's " Life," that she was resolved "*never again to be placed in his power.*" These words, which have been the cause of, if possible, still more horrible imputations against Byron even than the one brought by Mrs. Stowe, conclusively prove that her reason for refusing to live with him was not her belief in the truth of the latter. The question arises, Did she *at that time* entertain the belief at all? Had it as yet entered her head, or entered it except in the form of an incipient hallucination? We have seen that, *only two or three weeks previously*, she had christened her own child *Augusta* Ada, after the Hon. Mrs. Leigh, and it may therefore, we think, be safely assumed that she did not then so much as imagine that between Mrs. Leigh and her brother there existed more than a fond fraternal affection. But if the hallucination had not commenced when late in December, 1815, her babe was christened; nor yet in January, 1816, a fort-night or so later, when she firmly resolved, according to her own language, " never again to be placed in her husband's power," when did it begin? It has been said that Dr. Lushington can set this matter at rest; but a moment's reflection is enough to show that he can do nothing of the kind, any more than Mrs. Stowe can. All that he can do is to inform us—and this, I think, he ought to do—whether the story told by Lady Byron to Mrs. Stowe in 1856 is the same story that was told by her to him in 1816. Supposing that she told him a totally different story, there would then be an end of this story and every other one, and of Lady Byron's credit altogether. Supposing, however, that the two stories agree, obviously it will prove nothing more than that Lady Byron entertained the hallucination at the date of her interview with Mr. Lushington, and that Mr. Lushington chose to believe it as Gospel truth. But what was the date of this interview? Lady Byron quitted her husband on the 16th of January; but her interview with Mr. Lushington did not take place till considerably after. The precise date has never been stated; but a near approach to it may be arrived at from a letter written by Mr. Lushington, fourteen years later, at the request of Lady Byron. In that letter the following passage occurs:—

"When you came to town, in about a fortnight, or perhaps more, after my first interview with Lady Noel, I was, for the first time, informed by you of facts utterly unknown, as I have no doubt, to Sir Ralph and Lady Noel."

Now, here we have a not precisely stated, but clearly a considerable amount of time accounted for between

the time that Lady Byron quitted her husband, "resolved
never again to be placed in his power," and the communication, even supposing it to be in agreement with
the statement recorded by Mrs. Stowe, made by her to
Mr. Lushington. For among them they had first tried
to make out that Lord Byron was mad. Failing in that,
not Lady Byron, but her mother, instructed by her,
sought an interview with Mr. Lushington, for the avowed
purpose of obtaining an opinion from him that a separation was indispensable. He has left it on record that,
instructed so far, he thought a separation not at all indispensable. Not till *about a fortnight or more later*, when
Lady Byron, fearing to be "placed again in her husband's
power," as she says, herself saw Mr. Lushington, and told
him something fresh—in fact, something quite different
from what she had instructed her mother to tell him—
did he declare a reconciliation impossible.

Now, had the hallucination grown up in the considerable interval that elapsed between her resolving never to
live with her husband again, and the moment when she
discovered that the reasons she alleged for refusing to do
so were declared to be insufficient? Had she been
dwelling upon what she thought her wrongs, and trying
to account satisfactorily to her own *amour propre* for
what she esteemed her husband's want of consideration
and devotion to her, and in a sense for the *spreta forma*,
which he was bound never in any way to treat with injury

or neglect? Had she, moreover, whilst herself urging reasons that were declared to be insufficient, got wind of one of the thousand guesses that were being made by public curiosity all on fire to know what was the real sufficient reason for her refusal to return to him? Was the hallucination first suggested to her by her desire to account for his other alleged treatment of her, by nasty rumour, by her resolve never to live with him again, or by all these three combined? If the hallucination really existed at this time, that, no doubt, must be the true account of its origin. If it took its rise later on, the matter becomes simpler still. Rumour, fostered by Lady Byron's dogged silence, attributed every crime conceivable to her husband—incest, it would seem, among the number; and once thus possessed of the hallucination, every word and incident in Byron's past and future life would but strengthen it. Mrs. Stowe credits Lady Byron with a "supernatural sense of moral divination," and it is quite clear that Mrs. Stowe's catalogue of Lady Byron's qualities was obtained from Lady Byron herself. This belief in a supernatural sense of divination would naturally make her infallible in her own eyes. Then came "Manfred;" then came "Cain;" then came the stanzas to Augusta; and Lady Byron, arguing like Mrs. Stowe—and no doubt Mrs. Stowe got the argument from Lady Byron—would feel that anybody who read them with the belief that Lord Byron had

committed incest with his sister, would see plainly that
he must have done so. The hallucination would grow
with years, until—crowning statement of all!—Lady
Byron's supernatural sense of moral divination enabled
her to know that a child of Mrs. Leigh's—Mrs. Leigh
being a married woman, having other children, and living
with her husband the whole time—was " an unfortunate
child of sin, born with a curse upon her, and with
abnormal propensities to evil in it," and to pick it out
and watch over it till death took the responsibility out of
her hands. Here we reach the climacteric of the fabulous. Yet it is evident, from Mrs. Stowe's own account,
that Lady Byron believed this part of the fable, too, and
cherished it more than all the rest.

It is really wonderful that all the time so much debate
has been held as to whether Byron was likely to commit
incest, nobody has dreamed of asking, Was Mrs. Leigh
likely to commit it? Yet obviously this is an important
question, and one very different from the same inquiry
as applied to her brother. Nobody can point at the
" wild fame of *her* ungoverned youth ;" and the only
record that she has left of her sentiments on morals is her
determination, to which we have already alluded, not to
read " Don Juan " because it was so much abused on that
score. I will print just one letter written by her, and the
reader can then judge for himself what sort of person
she probably was. To my thinking it speaks volumes.

"St. J. P., Aug., 1838.

"Dear Mr. ———,—It is an age since I have written to you; the fact is, I have been ashamed to do so, or else too unhappy, and if you knew how much so, I think you would forgive me. I write now because I would not have you think I forgot your kindness, or that I was unmindful of my own omission. All that I can say is, that it has been quite out of my power to liquidate your claims on me, and very unhappy it makes me. My only hope is on some arrangement I contemplate with my eldest son; but such things take time. Dear Mr. ———, it is impossible to describe to you what I have suffered for some years. I must be composed of lead to be alive! At this moment I have more than enough of anxiety to kill a host. For three, out of six remaining children, I am in the most overwhelming solicitude, and without that which could alone remedy in two instances, and mitigate in a third. There is always much to be thankful for if one will seek for it, and I desire to be thankful for my many blessings, and resigned and patient under the dispensation of my life. I will not be so selfish as to dwell upon them. This letter is indeed written in the spirit of anxiety for what you must think of me. I fear you are angry, and yet I know I could not possibly help the cause. Heaven grant that I may ere long. I hope you and yours are as well as I wish, and if you would write and tell me about you all I should be very glad, for I can never cease to feel an interest on the subject or grateful for all your kindness to yours most truly obliged,

"AUG. LEIGH."

It is obvious that at this period she, at least, was not benefiting by that general benevolence of Lady Byron's of which we have heard so much, and which Mrs. Stowe informs us that Mrs. Leigh—having repented !—received from Lady Byron in her last sickness and dying hours. Yet in 1820 she was apparently in occasional commu-

nication with Lady Byron; for Byron says in a letter to
Murray :—

"*Pray tell Mrs. Leigh to request Lady Byron to urge forward
the transfer from the funds.* I wrote to Lady Byron on business
this post, addressed to the care of Mr. D. Kinnaird."

Here is an additional element of difficulty in this story,
for we find Lady Byron *as late as* 1820 in communication
with Mrs. Leigh, and likely to be influenced by her. In
1838, however, though she still has her £7,000 a year,
and no champion of Greek independence to help her to
spend it, she allows Mrs. Leigh to live in poverty and
debt, and to be so overwhelmed with money anxieties
and miseries as to be compelled to say, in language
reminding one strongly of what her brother would have
used, that "she must be composed of lead to be
alive"!

And this brings me to a question which, after all that
has been said against Lord Byron and in favour of his
wife, I have no intention of leaving untouched. This is
the real character of Lady Byron. She is supposed to
have been a saint. Mrs. Stowe, the editor of *Macmillan*,
and scores of other pious enthusiasts, say that she was
"divine." Let us see some proof of her "divinity."
The following facts have been contributed to the controversy by no less well-known and trustworthy a person
than Mr. William Howitt, and I reproduce them
textually here :—

" I knew her for some years, and visited her at her house in town, at her summer residence at Richmond, at Esher, and met her at her son-in-law, Lord Lovelace's, at Ockham. She also visited us at Esher and Highgate. I am sure that Lady Byron was a woman of the most honourable and conscientious intentions, but she was subject to a constitutional idiosyncrasy of a most peculiar kind, which rendered her, when under its influence, absolutely and persistently unjust. I am quite sure from my own observations of her that, when seized by this peculiar condition of the nerves, she was helplessly under its control. Through this the changes in her mood were sudden, and most painful to all about her. I have seen her of an evening in the most amiable, cordial, and sunny humour, full of interest and sympathy; and I have seen her the next morning come down as if she had lain all night not on a feather-bed, but on a glacier—frozen as it were to the very soul, and no efforts on the part of those around her could restore her for the day to a genial social warmth. In such moments she seemed to take sudden and deep impressions against persons and things, which, though the worst might pass away, left a permanent effect. Let me give an instance or two.

" Lady Byron was, at the period I speak of, deeply interested in the establishment of working schools for the education of children of the labouring classes. She induced Lord Lovelace to erect one at Ockham; she built one on her estate at Kirby Mallory, in Leicestershire. On one occasion, in one of her most amiable moods, she asked me to lunch with her in town, that we might discuss her plans for this system of education. She promised to arrange that we should not be interrupted for some hours. I went at the time fixed; but, to my consternation, found her in one of her frozen fits. The touch of her hand was like that of death; in her manner there was the silence of the grave. We sat down to luncheon by ourselves, and I endeavoured to break the ice by speaking of incidents of the day. It was in vain. The devil of the North Pole was upon her, and I could only extract icy monosyllables. When we returned to the drawing-room I sought to interest her in the topic on which we had met, and which she had so truly at heart. It was hopeless.

She said she felt unable to go into it, and I was glad to get away.

"Again, she was in great difficulty as to the selection of a master for her working school at Kirby Mallory. It was necessary for him to unite the very rarely united qualities of a thoroughly practical knowledge of the operations of agriculture and gardening with the education and information of an accomplished schoolmaster. She asked me to try and discover this *rara avis* for her. I knew exactly such a man in Nottinghamshire, who was at the same time thoroughly honourable, trustworthy, and fond of teaching. At her earnest request I prevailed on him to give up his then comfortable position and accept her offer. For a time he was everything in her eyes that a man and a schoolmaster could be. She was continually speaking of him when we met in the most cordial terms. But in the course, as I remember, of two or three years, the poor fellow wrote to me in the utmost distress, saying that Lady Byron, without the slightest intimation of being in any way dissatisfied with him, or with his management of the school, had given him notice to quit. He had entreated her to let him know what was the cause of this sudden dismissal. She refused to give any, and he entreated me to write to her and endeavour to remove her displeasure, or to ascertain its cause. I felt, from what I had seen of Lady Byron before, that it was useless. I wrote to him, 'Remember Lord Byron! If Lady Byron has taken into her head that you shall go, nothing will turn her. Go you must, and you had better prepare for it.' And the poor fellow, with a family of about five children, and his old situation filled up, turned out into the world to comparative ruin."

So much for Lady Byron as painted by an impartial hand. Now for a glimpse of her as painted by a partial hand—her own :—

"I am a very incompetent judge of the impression which the last canto of 'Childe Harold' may produce on the minds of indifferent readers. It contains the usual trace of a conscience restlessly awake, though his object has been too long to aggravate its burden, as if it could thus be oppressed into eternal stupor. I will hope, as you do, that it survives for his ultimate good. It was the acuteness of his remorse, impenitent in its character, which so long seemed to demand from my compassion to spare every semblance of reproach, every look of grief, which might have said to his conscience, 'You have made me wretched.' I am decidedly of opinion that he *is* responsible. He has wished to be thought partially deranged, or on the brink of it, to perplex observers and prevent them from tracing effects to their real causes through all the intricacies of his conduct. I was, as I told you, at one time the dupe of his acted insanity, and clung to the former delusions in regard to the motives that concerned me personally till the whole system was laid bare. He is the absolute monarch of words, and uses them, as Buonaparte did lives, for conquest, without more regard to their intrinsic value, considering them only as ciphers which must derive all their import from the situation in which he places them, and the ends to which he adapts them, with such consummate skill. Why, then, you will say, does he not employ them to give a better colour to his own character? Because he is too good an actor to over-act, or to assume a moral garb which it would be easy to strip off. In regard to his poetry egotism is the vital principle of his imagination, which it is difficult for him to kindle on any subject with which his own character and interests are not identified; but by the introduction of fictitious incidents, by change of scene or time, he has enveloped his poetical disclosures in a system impenetrable except to a very few, and his constant desire of creating a sensation makes him not averse to be the object of wonder and curiosity, even though accompanied by some dark and vague suspicions. Nothing has contributed more to the misunderstanding of his real character than the lonely grandeur in which he shrouds it, and his affectation of being above mankind, when he exists almost in their voice. The romance of his sentiments is another feature of this mask of state. I know no one more habitually destitute of that enthusiasm he so beautifully expresses, and to which he can work up his fancy chiefly by contagion. I had heard he was the best of brothers, the most generous of friends, and I thought such feelings only required to be warmed and cherished into more diffusive benevolence. Though these opinions are eradicated, and could never return but with the decay of my memory, you will not wonder if there are still moments when the association of feelings which arose from them soften and sadden my thoughts."

Mrs. Stowe, and folks of her calibre, may, if they like, consider these the utterances of "divine love," "supernatural charity," and more than human forbearance. But any impartial man or woman of the world will pronounce them to be the words of self-righteous and unsympathising Pharisaism. Byron may have been a publican and a sinner; but his wife completes the scriptural picture. Worse than that. In these words, *written by herself*, malignity is unmistakably apparent to any dispassionate judge. Yet she may, as Mrs. Stowe declares, have at last relented towards poor Mrs. Leigh, who had committed the heinous fault of sticking to her own flesh and blood in the agony of his greatest misfortune; and we can easily understand how, impelled by that passionate fondness for piety and for power which are so often found in combination, she thoroughly enjoyed heaping coals of fire on the unconscious head of such terrible sinners as poor Mrs. Leigh and the child that had manifestly on its soul the curse of sin!

Mrs. Stowe sees—and Lady Byron saw—clearly enough, that for the "True Story" to be believed, Byron must never have loved his wife either as Miss Milbanke or as Lady

Byron. I could fill pages with the proofs that he unques-
tionably did so, both before his marriage, after his marriage,
and after the separation. Lady Melbourne, his friend—
" when I say friend," he writes, " I mean *not* mistress, for
that's the antipode " (yet his sister, his "best friend,"
was his mistress, forsooth !)—could testify, were she yet
alive, to his quite boyish love for Miss Milbanke when
she at last accepted him. That they were unhappy together is certain ; and equally certain that they were much
better apart. But her refusal to let him return to her it
was that drove him into his worst excesses. The peculiarly
defiant tone of his letters is as apparent as is the defiant
course of his morality, during the time which elapsed
between the year he spent, immediately after the separation, in trying to bring about a reconciliation, and the
period when, restored to his better senses, he felt convinced that the Countess Guiccioli loved him, and he
gave himself *wholly* to her. No doubt she has written a
not very wise book ; but she behaved nobly to Byron ;
she was an Italian, the victim of Italian manners and
morals, which are quite different from our own ; and all
Englishmen of right feeling abstain from harsh words
against her. After her influence fell upon Byron, even
the irritating remembrances of the past could not drive
him to fresh excesses. " Everybody could manage my
lord," said Fletcher, "*except my lady*." No man, moreover, it may be added, ever had better or truer friends,

and their testimony alone is almost conclusive against Mrs. Stowe's story.    Let one instance suffice.    A " Citizen of the United States " has given the following evidence :—

" I was for many years on terms of the closest intimacy with three men who knew more than almost any others of Byron's personal character and history, and who happened to be precisely the men who were concerned in, or had special knowledge of, the destruction of his autobiography.    I speak of Moore, Rogers, and Luttrell, two of whom were actually parties to the destruction of the manuscript.    From 1845 to 1852 (when I left England) I was in constant communication with all the three, or rather with the two who still survived (Luttrell died in 1851, and Moore early in 1852).    I have repeatedly heard conversations among them as to the causes of Byron's separation from his wife, and have again and again heard Mr. Moore speak of the character and purport of the memoir, and of the motives which induced him to permit its destruction.    He had been so hotly censured for what was considered his weakness in the matter, that he often spoke at much length about it in his own defence ; and—while he always insisted that the memoir was disfigured by occasional outbreaks of petulance or anger, and filled with many details which, though insignificant, were calculated to cause annoyance to persons still living—he spoke in a way to convince any hearer that the memoir concealed no ' dark and terrible secret,' and that he, at least, had never derived, either from that memoir or from his intimate knowledge of all the parties and their surroundings, the remotest hint of any such horror as is now declared to be freshly unveiled ; and I am perfectly certain that the same may be said as to Rogers and Luttrell."

All this, however, Mrs. Stowe asserts, and Lady Byron asserted, is but the result of Byron's extraordinary powers of dissimulation.    Indeed, according to them, his life

was one long acted lie; and notably whenever he
referred to his wife, whom he hated, injured, and then
strove systematically to misrepresent, by simulating feelings of which he was quite incapable.     His writings
overflow with references to his love for her, and to her
implacability towards him.    All these, Mrs. Stowe says,
were deliberate lies, set some in the most majestic, some
in the most pathetic verse in the language, but mere part
and parcel of a life of sustained hypocrisy.

Let us turn to Moore.    He says he was strongly
inclined, on first reading the famous " Farewell," to
regard it rather as a work of art and fancy than anything more real :—

" On reading, however," he continues, " Byron's own account
of all the circumstances in the memoranda, I found that on this
point, in common with a large portion of the public, I had done
him injustice.  He there described, in a manner whose sincerity
there was no doubting, the swell of tender recollections under the
influences of which, as he sat one night musing in his study, these
stanzas were produced—the tears, as he said, falling fast over the
paper as he wrote them.  The appearance of the MS. confirms
this account of the circumstances under which it was written.
Neither did it appear to have been from any wish or intention of his
own, but through the injudicious zeal of a friend whom he had
suffered to take a copy, that the verses met the public eye."

Such an absolute demonstration of the sincerity of his
feelings cannot be expected in every instance; but it is
pretty certain that, were there even no other evidence
than that of his writings to rebut the charge of his hating

his wife and labouring by brutality to get rid of her in order to gratify an incestuous passion for his sister, they alone would stand like impenetrable guardian spirits between his grave and the abominable aspersion Mrs. Stowe strains every nerve to inscribe on it. But the story, as we have seen, besides brimming over with gross improbabilities, is full of utterly irreconcilable inconsistencies, and is born with the stamp of death upon it. To the end of time Byron and his verse will be among the most cherished possessions of mankind; and if posterity deigns to preserve the memory of this foul fable in connection with his name, it will be only to remember that it was concocted by a woman of a very peculiar temperament and not gifted with a very fine sense of justice, first publicly narrated by an American writer of romances, published by a magazine somewhat in need of notoriety, accepted for a moment by the prurient and the incurable lovers of scandal, but after due scrutiny and just reflection entirely repudiated by the definitive voice of an offended people.

P.S.—*Vide* Appendix.

# APPENDIX.

A.—Lady Byron has left us some exceedingly candid, if not very consistent, accounts of the opinion she formed of her husband. It is only fair we should have his opinion of her. Shortly before he died, he gave it in the following written words :—

"Lady Byron's letters were always enigmatical, often unintelligible. She was easily made the dupe of the designing, for she thought her knowledge of mankind infallible. She had got some foolish idea of Madame de Staël's into her head, that a person may be better known in the first hour than in ten years. She had the habit of drawing people's characters after she had seen them once or twice. She wrote pages and pages on my character, but it was as unlike as possible. She was governed by what she called fixed rules and principles, squared mathematically. It must be confessed, however, that she gave no proof of her boasted consistency. First she refused me, then she accepted me, then she separated herself from me—so much for consistency."

I fancy all impartial people will be disposed to think that this is a view both more sensible, accurate, and charitable than the one which—except, of course, in her "divine" moments—she took of him.

B.—The following highly valuable testimony, obtained too late to insert in the body of the foregoing "Vindication," may figure fitly here. The writer is the Dowager

Lady S——, a lady described as " of great natural abilities, unimpaired by advanced age (eighty-two), and whose knowledge of the world—fashionable, political, and literary—both of days long past and of these, is unsurpassed." She says :—

" We have a great subject of interest in Mrs. Stowe's account of Lord Byron. I want to know the truth. I have seen a great deal of Mrs. Leigh (Augusta), having passed some days with her and Colonel Leigh, for my husband's shooting is near Newmarket, when Lord Byron was in the house, and, as she told me, was writing ' The Corsair,' to my great astonishment, for it was a wretched small house, full of her ill-trained children, who were always running up and down stairs and going into ' uncle's ' bed-room, where he remained all the morning. Mrs. Leigh was like a mother to Byron, being so much older, and not at all an attrac-tive person. I afterwards went with her, at her request, to pay a wedding visit to Lady Byron when she returned to town, and she (Mrs. Leigh) expressed the greatest anxiety that his marriage should reform him. He opened the drawing-room door himself, and re-ceived my congratulations as savagely as I expected, looking demon-like, as he often did. But my astonishment at the present accusation is unbounded. She, a Dowdy-Goody, I being then, I suppose, a young fine lady. Scrope Davis used to come to dinner, and talked to me a great deal about Byron afterwards, when he resided in the country, and I never remember a hint at this un-natural and improbable *liaison* when all London was at Byron's feet. I have heard from Lady A—— I——, relative to ——, and to Mrs. Leigh, that my recollection of her was perfectly cor-rect. She says, ' She was an amiable and devoted wife, and mother of seven children. Her husband was very fond of her, and had a high opinion of her. She must have been married (in 1807) when Byron was quite a boy (he was 19). She had no taste for poetry. She had sad misfortunes in her later years. Her excellent and only surviving daughter nursed her with the tenderest affection in her last illness. How any one could have been so wicked as to write so horrible a story of one too long dead to have friends left who could refute the story, seems beyond belief.' "

C.—The following letter, which has reached me at the last moment of going to press, confirms, in every particular, the view maintained by me, in the face of much incredulity, from the very first moment that I sat down to write the " Vindication." Taken in conjunction with Mr. Howitt's letter, it would seem to be conclusive as to the existence of Lady Byron's hallucinations :—

" Sir,—Lady Noel Byron resided, on and off, many years in Brighton, and her circle of friends coincided very closely with my own. For most of these years I heard but of one crime of which she accused her dead husband, but latterly of two, which need not be named. Six or seven persons, more or less known to me, received her communications, three of whom were Americans. Her communications were not given as secrets, but, on the contrary, as facts to be used for the defence of her conduct, character, or memory. Some of these persons received them as Mrs. Beecher Stowe did—the Rev. Frederick Robertson for one; others thought 'her mind was touched upon the subject of the separation.' In 1847 one of her best friends asked me to talk with her on the liabilities to error of private judgment when deciding questions involving criminal charges which can be properly investigated only by public tribunals. No one, I told her, had a right to repeat such charges, except as decisions of courts of law. Her stories differed. Her narratives and memoranda were given away right and left. The confidantes who knew her best, her peculiarities, her troubles with her daughter, her elder grandson, her servants, never would have repeated her stories with pens and types. They thought her mind was touched. Suspicions had become delusions. Three of her friends, myself being one, came separately to this conclusion. The sealed papers held by her trustees, if they contain the accusations she made, can only be records of her delusions; for the charge she made most frequently is not capable of proof; and the charge Mrs. Stowe has published is comparatively recent, and utterly incredible. " JOHN ROBERTSON.

" 12, Norfolk Road, Sept. 12, 1869."

Perhaps the *Saturday Review* now understands what that word means.

VIRTUE AND CO., PRINTERS, CITY ROAD, LONDON.

www.ingramcontent.com/pod-product-compliance
Lightning Source LLC
Chambersburg PA
CBHW032044090426
42733CB00030B/651